CHILLERS 3

Mill View

The Bonfire

by Sandra Woodcock

Published in association with the Adult Literacy
and Basic Skills Unit

Hodder & Stoughton
LONDON SYDNEY AUCKLAND TORONTO

The publishers and ALBSU wish to acknowledge the contribution of the NEWMAT
Project, Nottinghamshire Local Education Authority, and of the Project Leader,
Peter Beynon, in the conception, writing and publication of the *Chillers* series.

British Library Cataloguing in Publication Data
Woodcock, Sandra
  Mill view. The bonfire.–(Chillers: 3).
  1. English language – Readers
  I. Title   II. National Institute of Adult Education (England and Wales), *Adult
  Literacy and Basic Skills Unit*   III. Series
  428.6

ISBN 0 340 52104 X

First published 1989

© 1989 Adult Literacy and Basic Skills Unit

Typeset by Gecko Ltd, Bicester, Oxon
Printed for the educational publishing division of Hodder and Stoughton Ltd,
Mill Road, Dunton Green, Sevenoaks, Kent by St Edmundsbury Press Ltd,
Bury St Edmunds, Suffolk

Mill View

Ashdale is a beautiful place.
You might go there for a day out –
a picnic or a long walk, fresh air, wonderful views.
But as we drive along the side of the River Ash
and into the village,
I begin to shudder.
Ashdale is my home,
but it's been a place of horror for me.

It started a few months ago.
I saw a job advert in the village Post Office:

> **WANTED**
> Reliable woman to
> help in the house.
> Working Couple
> Mill View Cottage.

Mill View Cottage is about a mile out of the village.
It's close to the river.
As you can tell from the name,
it overlooks an old cotton mill.

I telephoned about the job
and was asked to go up there the next day.

It didn't take long on my bike.
I had been past the cottage many times.
It had been empty for some time.
Now some people had moved in.
It looked better.

I left my bike just inside the gate
and walked slowly up the garden path.
It was June.
The garden had been neglected.
It was wild
with the roses and hollyhocks all over the place.

I looked up to the little windows
and saw the face of a small child.
Good! I liked children.
I knocked at the door and waited.

It was Marian Winter who opened the door.
I disliked her on sight.
She was like her name – cold and unfriendly.
Her husband Harry wasn't any better.
But the work seemed easy and the pay was good.
I took the job.

'You'll be here by yourself most of the time,'
Marian had said.
'We both work full-time.'

Then I remembered.
'Does someone look after your son?'
They looked at each other.
Then Marian snapped, 'We don't have children.
Please be here at 9 a.m. on Monday.
That's all.'
She turned away.

Outside the front door I felt cold
even though it was a warm summer day.
What an odd couple!

The first two weeks went well.
I liked working at the cottage.
I felt at home there.
It was cosy and interesting – unlike its owners.

I didn't see much of Marian Winter
and nothing of her husband.
I dismissed the memory of the child's face.
It must have been a trick of the light,
or me daydreaming!

Then one Wednesday morning
I was dusting in the dining room when I heard it –
the sound of a child crying, sobbing.
It was quite clear.
I dropped the duster and ran into the next room.
No one there! Upstairs then? Nothing!

I ran from room to room.
There was no sign of a child anywhere.
The crying had stopped.

Two days later I heard it again.
This time
it seemed to come from outside the house.
I went into the garden.

In one corner there were a few outbuildings –
a shed, an old store, a wash-house.
Something seemed to draw me
towards the wash-house.
I felt a rush of cold air.
Then I thought I saw a child's face at the window.
I went closer and peered inside.

Through the mist of dirt and cobwebs
on the window, I saw a child.
He was perhaps seven or eight.
He had a tiny pale face with a look of agony,
and dark shadows under huge eyes.
His body was thin and bent like that of an old man.
As I watched, the child bent down
and crawled on the floor like an animal.
Then he stared right into my eyes and smiled.
But the smile was horrific.
The child's teeth were sharp and pointed
like those of a dog or a wolf.
I backed away in horror.

The door was locked.
I banged on it with both fists
but I knew it was hopeless.
And then I was frightened.
What was going on here?
The Winters had a child locked away!
All sorts of wild ideas ran through my mind –
newspaper stories of children neglected,
abused, tortured.
I couldn't stand it.
Marian and Harry Winter –
were they really that evil?

Shaking and sobbing I ran to the house
and called the local police station.

Marian Winter had to face my wild story.
The wash-house was opened
for the police to investigate.
As I half expected, no one was there.
There were no signs
that a child had ever been inside.
The police looked all over the place.
Marian Winter spoke not a word to me,
but her icy stare seemed to cut right through me.

I was dismissed as a crazy woman
with an overworked imagination.
I felt like a naughty child,
but I knew that what I had seen
was not in my imagination.
That left only one possibility.
The child, if not real and not imagined,
must be a child of the spirit world –
a ghost from the past.

My time at the cottage had ended.
For my own sake
I had to stop thinking about what I had seen there –
but that wasn't easy.
I found it hard to sleep.
When I did sleep my dream was always the same –
a nightmare of the child's face.
I began to lose weight.
I lost interest in eating.
The child haunted me by day and by night.
I became very ill.
My sister had to come from Manchester.
She took me back to her house.

I had been living with my sister
for about three months,
when I had a letter from Marian Winter.
What she told me made it possible for me
to think of a normal life again.

She and her husband had begun work
to extend the cottage.
Workmen digging the foundations
for the extension
had uncovered the bones of a small child.
When examined, these bones were found
to be over a hundred years old. But not only that,
Marian Winter had seen the ghost-child herself!

Experts said that the bones were probably of a child
who had worked at the cotton mill
in the nineteenth century.
Many children, especially orphans,
were sent there to work and to live.
They were kept in terrible conditions.
Half starved, living like animals,
they ate revolting food.
Sometimes their teeth were filed
so they could eat very tough food.
Many of these children died –
too many to bury in the local graveyard
without a scandal.
So it was not unusual
to bury some of them elsewhere.
Part of the wasteland behind the mill
had become the garden of Mill Cottage.

Marian Winter then gave me
the most welcome invitation I have ever had.
She asked me to return to Ashdale
to witness the proper Christian burial
of those bones in the local churchyard.

The child was to be at peace . . . and so were we.

The Bonfire

'Hey, Dave! Are you going to the bonfire tonight?'
Flat on his back, under his motorbike,
Dave couldn't see who was shouting.
He dragged himself out and stood up.
It was Jeff from round the corner.

'Hello, Jeff. What bonfire?'
'At the pub in the next village – the Cranmer Arms.
There's a barbecue and fireworks. Should be good.
They've never had one at the pub before.'

Dave was thinking about it.
He didn't know many people yet.
They'd only moved in a few weeks ago.
'Maybe I'll go,' he said.
'Great. Do you want a lift? About 7.30?'
'No thanks,' said Dave. 'I can't make it till later.
I'll walk over. It's only just over a mile.'
'Right. See you there.'

It was nine o'clock
when Dave set off for the Cranmer Arms
in Aslockton.
It was a quiet road with fields on each side –
no houses until he reached the village.
But Dave enjoyed the walk
and the smell of the damp November night.
Bonfire Night!
It made him feel like a kid again.

Another ten minutes and he'd be there.
In the moonlight
he could see a house ahead of him.
People came out, heading for the village.

Suddenly Dave heard a sound.
He turned round.
There was a man behind him.
'Hi! Are you going to the bonfire?' Dave asked.
The man walked past him,
then stopped and looked around.
'Bonfire . . . yes . . .,' he said.
He had a strange, distant look on his face.
Maybe he wasn't sure where to go.
But anyone could find a bonfire
in a small place like this.
'It's in the field next to the pub,' Dave said.
'You can come with me if you like.'

Then, for something to say, he said,
'Do you know the village?'
The man seemed to be looking at something
a long way in front.
He didn't answer for a while.
Then he said, 'I was born here.'
He wasn't lost then.
'Well, I'm from the next village.
Dave Best's my name.'
The man stared at him.
Then he said slowly, 'My name is . . . Thomas . . .'

Dave shivered.
A grey November mist
had slipped down around him.
They were almost at the pub.
He could hear the shouting and singing
of people enjoying themselves.
'There's a good crowd here,' he said.
No reply.
Dave wanted to get away from this strange man.
He was beginning to feel creepy.
One last try.

'This mist's damp,' he said.
'But the fire should burn well
if they've got dry wood.'
The man was still silent – he looked almost afraid.
He began to mutter to himself.
Dave couldn't hear the words.
It sounded like 'Be brave. Be brave.'
He didn't make sense.

The lights from the pub windows
lit up the man's face –
a tired pale face.
Then he slowly lifted his right arm to cover his face,
as if the light was too bright.
Dave saw with horror
that the man's right hand
was covered in great raw blisters.
It looked as if it had been badly burned.

Dave ran into the pub garden.
He pushed past the laughing people.
He made straight for the bar.
'Double whisky.'

A few minutes later
he was sitting with Jeff and two of his mates.
The lights were bright.
The pub was alive with chattering people,
a different world from the road outside.

Dave felt warmer.
He began to relax
and take in what the others were saying.
They seemed to be talking about the pub –
how it had got its name.
Dave pricked up his ears.
'What's that you say?
It's named after a man called Thomas?'

'That's right,' Jeff said.
'Thomas Cranmer.
Burnt to death by Bloody Mary –
Queen Mary Tudor, I should say.'

'Burnt to death. . . !'
Dave couldn't believe what he was hearing.

Jeff was enjoying himself telling the story.
'Yes that's right. Burnt for his religion.
Couldn't become a Catholic
so Bloody Mary had him burnt.'

'His right hand . . .,' Dave was talking to himself.

'Oh you know about that,' Jeff said cheerfully.
The others looked puzzled.
'Well,' said Jeff.
'It seems that in prison,
our Thomas had signed a paper
to say he believed in the Catholic religion –
hoped to save his skin.
But he was sent to the fire anyway.
Then he was ashamed.
So as soon as they lit the fire
he put his right hand into the flames
so it would burn first.
The hand that signed the paper – see?'

Dave looked stunned.
Jeff slapped him on the back.
'Come on. Don't look like that.
It was hundreds of years ago, mate!
Tell you what . . .,' he grinned.
'It's a bit of a cheek
having a bonfire right here where he was born.
It's enough to make old Thomas turn in his grave.'